THE BIG BOOK OF MADAGASCAR FACTS

AN EDUCATIONAL COUNTRY TRAVEL PICTURE BOOK FOR KIDS ABOUT HISTORY, DESTINATION PLACES, ANIMALS, AND MANY MORE

D1524464

Unique Location: Madagascar is the fourth largest island in the world, located in the Indian Ocean off the southeastern coast of Africa.

Which continent does Madagascar belong to?
Madagascar is part of the African continent.

How big is Madagascar?
Madagascar is about 587,041 square kilometers (226,658 square miles) in size.
What percentage of the world's land does Madagascar occupy?
Madagascar occupies about 0.4% of the world's land area.

Which city is the largest in Madagascar?
The largest city in Madagascar is Antananarivo.
How many provinces does Madagascar have?
Madagascar has 6 provinces.

What is the population of Madagascar?
Madagascar has a population of approximately 31 million people.
Is Madagascar overly populated?
Madagascar is not considered overly populated; it has a relatively low population density.

What are the people of Madagascar called?
The people of Madagascar are called Malagasy.
What is Madagascar's literacy rate?
Madagascar's literacy rate is approximately 74.8%.

What is the national animal of Madagascar?
The national animal of Madagascar is the ring-tailed lemur.

What is the national bird of Madagascar?
The national bird of Madagascar is the Malagasy fish eagle.

What is the national sport of Madagascar?
The national sport of Madagascar is rugby.

What is the national tree of Madagascar?
The national tree of Madagascar is the Grandidier baobab.

What is the official name of Madagascar?
The official name of Madagascar is the Republic of Madagascar.
What is the currency of Madagascar?
The currency of Madagascar is the Malagasy Ariary.

How many time zones are there in Madagascar?
Madagascar has one time zone, East Africa Time (EAT).
What is Madagascar's nickname?
Madagascar is often nicknamed the "Red Island" due to its red soil.

Who ruled Madagascar first?
The first rulers of Madagascar were the Merina dynasty, which unified the island in the 19th century.

What is the oldest city in Madagascar?

The oldest city in Madagascar is likely Mahajanga (Majunga), which has a long history dating back to ancient times.

Which months are the coldest in Madagascar?
The coldest months in Madagascar are usually June and July.
Which months are the hottest in Madagascar?
The hottest months in Madagascar are typically January and February.

Why do tourists visit Madagascar?
Tourists visit Madagascar for its unique wildlife, beautiful landscapes, rainforests, beaches, and cultural experiences.

How many visitors visit Madagascar every year?
Madagascar receives about 300,000 to 400,000 visitors each year.

Biodiversity: Around 90% of the wildlife found in Madagascar is endemic, meaning they are not found anywhere else in the world.

Lemur Kingdom: Madagascar is famous for its lemurs, with over 100 different species and subspecies.

Baobab Trees: The island is home to six of the world's eight species of baobab trees.

Malagasy
French

Language: The official languages are Malagasy and French, but many people also speak English.

Tsingy de Bemaraha: This UNESCO World Heritage site features dramatic limestone formations known as tsingy.

Avenue of the Baobabs: A dirt road lined with towering baobab trees, this site is one of Madagascar's most famous landmarks.

Endangered Species: Many species, including the iconic lemur, are endangered due to habitat destruction.

Ranomafana National Park: This park is a biodiversity hotspot with numerous rare species of plants and animals.

Madagascar's Capital: The capital city is Antananarivo, often referred to as "Tana."

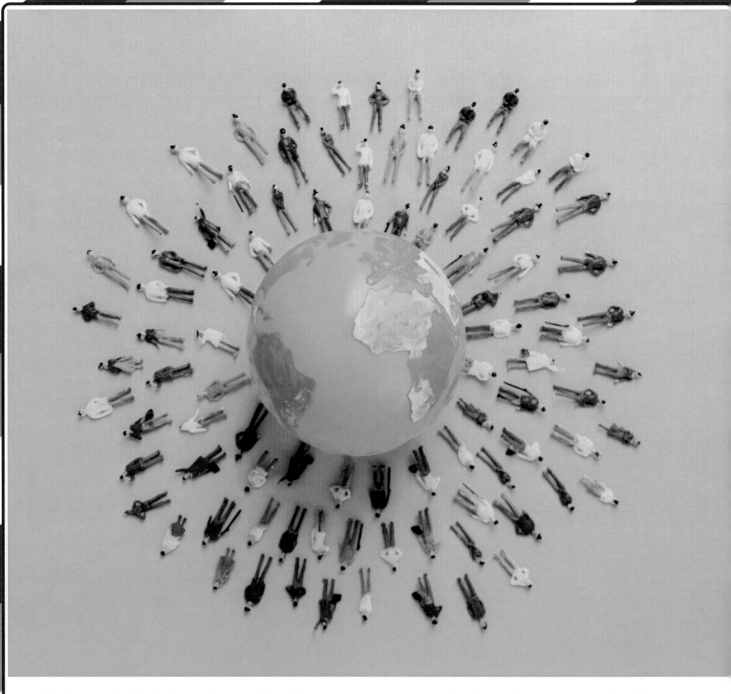

Cultural Melting Pot: Madagascar's population is a mix of African, Asian, and Arab descent.

Rice Cultivation: Rice is a staple food, and terraced rice paddies are a common sight.

Zebu Cattle: Zebu, a type of humped cattle, are an important part of Malagasy culture and economy.

Indri Lemur: The Indri, the largest living lemur, is known for its loud, distinctive calls.

Malagasy Cuisine: Traditional dishes often feature rice, zebu meat, seafood, and local spices.

Vanilla Production: Madagascar is one of the world's largest producers of vanilla.

Chameleons: The island has more species of chameleons than anywhere else on earth.

Ring-tailed Lemur: Easily recognizable by their long, striped tails, these lemurs are a favorite among visitors.

Isalo National Park: Known for its sandstone formations, deep canyons, and rich biodiversity.

Pirate History: In the 17th century, Madagascar was a haven for pirates, including the infamous Captain Kidd.

Cyclones: The island frequently experiences cyclones, especially during the rainy season from November to April.

Nosy Be: An island off the northwest coast, Nosy Be is a popular tourist destination known for its beaches and marine life.

Palace of the Queen: Rova of Antananarivo, a royal palace complex, offers insights into the island's history.

Education Challenges: Access to education is limited in many parts of Madagascar, with varying literacy rates.

Betsiboka River: Known for its dramatic red color due to heavy sediment load.

Amber Mountain: A national park with a tropical forest and abundant wildlife, located in the north.

Humpback Whales: These whales migrate to the waters near Madagascar for breeding and can be seen from June to September.

Rice Terraces: The highland areas are famous for their intricate rice terraces.

Moraingy: A traditional Malagasy martial art, practiced particularly in coastal regions.

Traditional Music: Malagasy music includes a variety of styles, with influences from Africa, Indonesia, and Europe.

Betsileo and Merina: The Merina and Betsileo are two of the prominent ethnic groups in Madagascar.

Madagascar Day Gecko: This vibrant green gecko is another of the island's unique reptiles.

Antsiranana Bay: A large, beautiful bay in the north, also known as Diego Suarez.

Madagascar Hissing Cockroach: One of the world's largest cockroach species, known for its distinctive hissing sound.

Lake Alaotra: The largest lake in Madagascar, an important habitat for the endangered Alaotra gentle lemur.

Spiny Forest: A unique ecosystem found in the southwest, characterized by its drought-resistant plants.

Malagasy Falconry: The use of birds of prey for hunting is a traditional practice in some regions.

Sea Turtles: Several species of sea turtles nest on Madagascar's beaches.

Red Sand Dunes of Irodo: Unique red sand dunes found in the north of Madagascar.

Bara People: Known for their cattle-herding culture and traditional way of life.

Kirindy Forest: A dry deciduous forest famous for its population of fossa, Madagascar's largest predator.

Local Markets: Markets, or "bazars," are a vibrant part of Malagasy culture where locals buy and sell goods.

Cave Exploration: The island has numerous caves, some with prehistoric significance and unique formations.

Mantasoa: A man-made lake and popular recreation area near Antananarivo.

Madagascar Fody: A small, brightly colored bird commonly seen throughout the island.

Hira Gasy: A traditional form of Malagasy theater that includes music, dance, and storytelling.

Clove Production: Madagascar is one of the leading producers of cloves in the world, accounting for approximately 10-15% of the global clove production.

Nosy Mangabe: A small island reserve known for its biodiversity and the rare Aye-aye lemur.

TOP 10 TRAVEL TIPS FOR VISITING MADAGASCAR:

1. **Learn Basic Malagasy Phrases:** Knowing some basic phrases in Malagasy can help you communicate better with locals and show respect for their culture.
2. **Carry Cash:** ATMs are not available everywhere, so it's good to have enough cash, especially in rural areas. The local currency is the Malagasy Ariary (MGA).
3. **Drink Bottled Water:** To avoid getting sick, drink only bottled or filtered water. Avoid ice in drinks unless you're sure it's made from safe water.
4. **Pack for Varied Weather:** Madagascar has different climates, so bring clothing for both hot and cool weather, and don't forget a rain jacket.
5. **Use Insect Repellent:** Protect yourself from mosquitoes by using insect repellent, wearing long sleeves, and sleeping under mosquito nets.
6. **Respect Local Customs:** Learn about and respect local customs and taboos (fady). This shows respect and helps you connect with the culture.
7. **Be Prepared for Slow Travel:** Roads can be rough and travel times longer than expected. Be patient and enjoy the journey.
8. **Hire Local Guides:** Local guides can enhance your experience by sharing their knowledge and helping you navigate the area safely.
9. **Respect Wildlife:** Madagascar's wildlife is unique and often endangered. Keep a safe distance, don't feed animals, and follow park rules.
10. **Stay in Eco-friendly Accommodations:** Support conservation efforts by choosing eco-friendly lodgings that promote sustainable tourism and protect the environment.

* * * * * * * * * * * * * * * * * * *Thank You* * * * * * * * * * * * * * * * * * *

Made in United States
North Haven, CT
20 August 2024

56298910R00024

Welcome to the enchanting island of Madagascar! Known for its incredible biodiversity, stunning landscapes, and unique culture, this island nation has something for everyone to discover. In this informative travel picture book, readers will explore the fascinating world of Madagascar, learning all about its geography, history, and customs.

Discover the home of the famous lemurs and the unique baobab trees, explore the vibrant markets of Antananarivo, and journey through the island's many charming villages and towns. Whether you're planning a trip to Madagascar or just want to learn more about this beautiful island, "The Big Book of Madagascar Facts" is the ultimate guide for readers of all ages.

ISBN 9798326154651